AF428954

I MissTea Time with Grandma

A STORY AND JOURNAL FOR GRIEF AND HEALING

Rev. Dr. JoBeth Kee-Rees LMFT

I Miss Tea Time with Grandma,
A STORY AND JOURNAL FOR GRIEF AND HEALING

Written by Rev. Dr. JoBeth Kee-Rees LMFT ©2024.
HealzOurHeartz, Austin, Texas,

llustrated by Sylvia LeDoux, ©2024
Edited by Hope Druckenmiller
thehopefuleditor.com

ISBN 979-8-9909443-0-5

All rights reserved.

I Miss Tea Time with Grandma

A STORY AND JOURNAL FOR GRIEF AND HEALING

Dear Parent or Caregiver,

First, I want to tell you that I am sorry for your loss. It is difficult to be grieving the death of a loved one and shepherd your child through the death of a loved one. I have also travelled this path of grieving and caregiving at the same time.

Second, please know that your child may be having a variety of feelings. They may feel angry, lonely, sad, scared, or worried. It is normal to have any or all these feelings right now. It is important to give them time and space to express those feelings. Connecting with you is one of the most important gifts you can give them right now. Go for a walk together, draw a picture together, talk about your favorite memories together, pray together. Grief needs to get out of the body. Grief needs to be expressed.

Third, please be patient with yourself and with your child. Grief is a journey. It is not something you can jump over. It is something you need to walk through. As you walk this journey of grief together, please know that all of us grieve in different ways. I encourage you to listen to your child. They will tell you what they need on their grief journey.

Finally, please know that I am praying for you and your child. I have walked this journey of grief with my children, and I know that healing can happen. Keep taking one step at a time on your grief journey. God is working in you and in your child. God is healing your hearts.

Blessings on your healing,

JoBeth

SHE LIKED TO DRINK TEA

As I stirred the roux

In the cast iron gumbo pot,

She drank hot tea as she said,

"keep stirring, a little longer…till it gets to the color of a pecan."

As she stirred the roux

In the cast iron gumbo pot,

She drank iced tea

To stay cool over the hot stove.

As she gazed

At the bright yellow orchids,

She drank hot tea

With her toast and plum jam.

As she rocked in her rocking chair,

She drank iced tea

And encouraged the oldest one

"Add a little more water, that one looks dry and thirsty."

When I felt joyful

We drank tea together

As her eyes sparkled and she said,

"Oh Sugar, I'm so happy for you!"

When I felt sad

We drank tea together

As she held my hand and said,

"I'm so sorry, I can't do much, but I can be here with you."

She laughed as she enjoyed her party

Afternoon high tea

With fancy hats, sandwiches, tea cakes

And, of course, hot tea.

On the day before she died,

I made a cup of hot tea for Grandma.

We visited at the kitchen table.

Her gentle eyes shimmered as she smiled.

Now, when my daughter feels sad,

we drink tea together.

I listen and say,

"Oh Honey, I'm so sorry, I will sit with you."

When she feels excited and joyful,

we drink tea together.

As I gaze at her, I smile and say,

"Honey, I'm so happy for you!"

To Mom, for inspiring in me… a love of storytelling and a taste for tea!

To Dad, for teaching me to have… a compassionate heart and a love of good gumbo!

PART 1

My Loved One,
Grandma

Dear Friend,

I wrote this book to remember my special person who died, Grandma. Her name was Reberta, and she was 100 years old when she died. We liked to drink tea together.

I also wrote this book for you. Who was your special person who died? What was their name? I hope this book helps you remember your loved one.

Your Friend,

JoBeth

Have you ever eaten gumbo? My favorate part is the shrimp!

Grandma loved to make a gumbo.

She taught my mother, and then me, how to cook the roux.

First, you melt the butter and toss in the flour, stirring constantly, as it becomes a blond roux and then a

caramel roux… 'keep stirring, don't let it burn!'

As I stirred the roux

In the cast iron gumbo pot,

She drank hot tea as she said,

"keep stirring, a little longer…till it gets to the color of a pecan."

Grandma lived an amazing life! She grew up in a Cajun family in southeast Texas. Her father was an oil field worker and a farmer. Her mother cooked for their 4 children. Sometimes she asked Reberta, the oldest girl, to help her stir the roux in the gumbo pot.

As she stirred the roux

In the cast iron gumbo pot,

She drank iced tea

To stay cool over the hot stove.

After Grandma and Grandpa raised their 2 children, they moved to Belize in Central America. In the warm wet tropical climate, Grandma loved to grow orchids. After she tended to her orchids high in the tree, she came inside to have breakfast with Grandpa.

As she gazed

At the bright yellow orchids,

She drank hot tea

With her toast and plum jam.

When Grandma turned 90 years old, she came to live with my parents in Texas. Rocking and visiting on the porch were some of her favorite activities. She still loved her flowers, and she taught her great-grand-children how to care for her amaryllis flowers on the back porch.

As she rocked in her rocking chair,

She drank iced tea

And encouraged the oldest one

"Add a little more water, that one looks dry and thirsty."

Grandma was a good listener. We often visited at the kitchen table. With the gumbo pot bubbling on the stove and a glowing fire in the fireplace, we sat down at the table to visit.

When I felt joyful

We drank tea together

As her eyes sparkled and she said,

"Oh Sugar, I'm so happy for you!"

When I felt sad

We drank tea together

As she held my hand and said,

"I'm so sorry, I can't do much, but I can be here with you."

Grandma loved to celebrate! When she turned 99, we had a double party for her. Her grandsons grilled and made a Texas barbeque. Her granddaughters got out the fancy china. We created an English Afternoon Tea to remember her years living in Belize.

She laughed as she enjoyed her party

Afternoon high tea

With fancy hats, sandwiches, tea cakes

And, of course, hot tea.

One winter afternoon, I went to visit. Grandma and Mom were talking and smiling in their chairs.

One of her great-grandsons was sitting on her lap. He was 6 years old, and she was 100 years old. They

rocked and laughed together.

On the day before she died,

I made a cup of hot tea for Grandma.

We visited at the kitchen table.

Her gentle eyes shimmered as she smiled.

Grandma taught me how important it is to spend time with loved ones.

I will always remember tea time with Grandma.

I continue what she taught me by sharing stories and tea on the back porch with my daughter

Now, When my daughter feels sad,

We drink tea together.

I listen and say,

"Oh Honey, I'm so sorry, I will sit with you."

When she feels excited and joyful,

We drink tea together.

As I gaze at her, I smile and say,

"Honey, I'm so happy for you!"

PART 2

YOUR LOVED ONE

The second part of the book is about you and your loved one who died. You can read it with someone and talk about your loved one. You can also do some of the activities by yourself and have some quiet time.

It is ok to feel happy and laugh sometimes. It is ok to feel sad and cry sometimes. You might also feel angry, guilty, or scared. It is normal to have these feelings right now.

Your grief, your feelings, need to get out of your body to heal. There are many ways to let your feelings out of your body. You can write it out, paint it out, walk it out, run it out, cry it out, talk it out, or pray it out. This journal can help you let you feelings out of your body.

Sometimes it helps to talk to someone you trust about this person and share your memories together. Sometimes it helps to pray and talk to God about your special person. God loves you, and God is healing your heart.

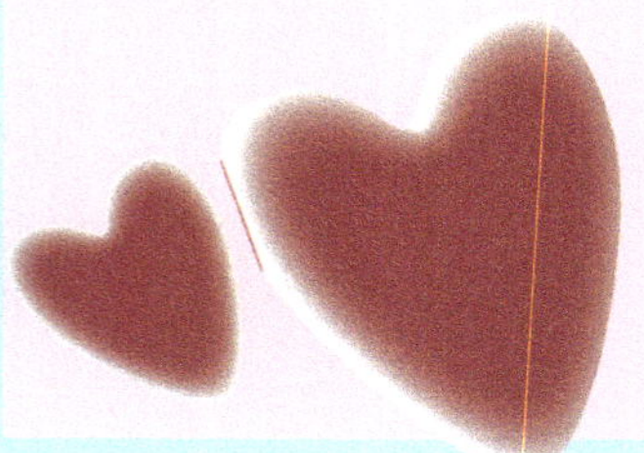

What was your special person's
favorite lunch or dinner?

I wonder…
what would it be like to eat
this meal and celebrate
your memories of the person who died?

What was your favorite thing to do
with your loved one
in the morning, or afternoon, or evening?

I wonder…
what would you like to do
each day to remember this person?
Would you like to go for a walk,
bake cookies,
read a story,
or something else?

What was your special person's
favorite flower or tree?

I wonder…
what would it be like
to plant a tree or grow a garden
in memory of this person?

What was your favorite thing to do with your loved one
in the spring, summer, fall, or winter?

I wonder…
what would you like to do each season
to remember this person?

Would you like to pick strawberries,
go swimming,
pick apples
play in the snow,
or something else?

What is one of your happy memories
about your special person?

What do you feel sad or miss about this person?

I wonder…
would you like to draw a picture
to remember the person who died?

As you think about your loved one,
is there anything you feel angry about?

Is there anything you feel worried about?

I wonder…
would you like to write
a letter or a poem
to remember this person?

Who can you talk to about your special person?

I wonder…
would you like to walk and talk?
Would you like a hug from them,
or something else?

What would you like God
to know about your loved one?

I wonder…
would you like to say a prayer
giving thanks for this person's life?
What would you like to say?

GRIEF AND HEALING JOURNEY
For the Caregiver

When a loved one dies, we are thrown onto a path that is painful and confusing. We are on a journey of grief and healing. Healing occurs in an environment that is emotionally safe. After the death or loss occurs, you can't change the loss, but you can choose how you respond to the loss. You and your child are on this journey together.

WHAT IS LOSS? Loss is the event; it is what happened. It can be the death of a family member, death of a pet, divorce of parents or of a friend's parent. Children experience loss in different ways depending upon their age. They all need to "tell the story", to talk about what happened from their perspective.

WHAT IS GRIEF? Grief is the feelings about the loss. We often feel sad during a loss because we miss our loved one. Sometimes we feel angry and ask "why". We might feel fear and wonder "could this happen again". We may feel guilty and blame ourselves. Sometimes an older child might feel relief if they watched a loved one suffer. Children may feel some or all of these feelings. They need the opportunity to express their feelings.

WHAT IS MOURNING? Mourning is what we do; it is a process. Grief has to get out of the body in order to heal. We can walk it out, run it out, write it out, draw it out, paint it out, talk it out, cry it out, hammer it out, garden it out, pray it out. It doesn't matter what activity you choose; it just has to get out of the body to heal. Listen to your child; they will tell you what they need.

HOW DOES HEALING HAPPEN? Healing occurs in several ways. Healing happens in the difficult moments; the painful feelings wash over you "like a wave". Even though the feelings are intense in the moment, they don't last forever. The feelings come, you feel them, and they go. You and your child have survived another wave of grief; you will survive many waves.

Healing happens in the everyday moments. You will notice moments of healing as you and your child savor the small everyday things together; as you notice the sunset and remember that your loved one enjoyed the sunset, as you taste the cinnamon in the cake and smile because your loved one liked cinnamon, as you drink tea and remember your loved one. As you have some quiet time by yourself or with your child, ask God to heal your hearts.

Healing happens in the big events, such as the first birthday or Christmas without the loved one. Spend time with your family and friends. You and your family may want to light a candle and tell stories about your loved one. You may want to say a prayer of thanks for the life of your loved one. Healing occurs when you go through these hard days together. You and your child will survive; you are healing.

ACKNOWLEDGEMENTS

There are so many of you to thank!

To Sylvia, this book would not exist without your inspiring colorful illustrations and your keen eye for design and formatting. Thank you from the bottom of my heart! To Hope, my niece, your encouragement from the first time you saw the manuscript to your expert editing skills mean the world to me. To Thomas, your technical skills and support as we built out the website for the book was incredibly helpful. To Stacy, Jeanie, and Jean Kay, thank you for saying yes and for your thoughtful, creative, and enthusiastic reviews.

To cousins, Dennis, Ben, Jimmy, and Lee, I have loved sharing a grandma, sharing holidays, and sharing numerous laughs with you; your joie de vivre is infectious. To siblings, Jennifer, David, John, Ellen, and Hollie, thank you for your love and encouragement. I'm so glad I get to travel the road of life with all of you. To Sophia and Luke, thank you for your love and your trust in me as we have walked through many losses and healing together. You inspire me every day to be a better mom and person. To my husband, Jim, thank you for your love, for holding my hand during sad times, for celebrating with me during joyful times, and for your boundless enthusiasm and ideas during this long writing/editing/publishing process. I love you with all my heart!

www.ingramcontent.com/pod-product-compliance
Lightning Source LLC
Chambersburg PA
CBHW040151110726
48005CB00018B/2721